Commitment Statement

I, the undersigned, here and now, commit to completing at least 80% of the experiences proposed in this book.

I firmly believe that every activity, from the simplest to the most adventurous, is an opportunity to strengthen my connection with myself, to explore new dimensions of my life beyond the work that defined me for so many years, and to build a precious treasure of memories for the future.
I embrace this journey with trust and determination, fully aware that every step, no matter how small, can enrich my life
in unexpected ways.

signature _____ date _____

signature _____ date _____

1. To go on a pic-nic

Date __/__/____

Place _____

Description of the moment _____

_____

_____

_____

Liking

Unforgettable Photo

it Again? | yes | | maybe | | no |

2. Netflix night at home

Date __/__/____

Place _____

Description of the moment _____

_____

_____

_____

Liking

Unforgettable Photo

it Again? | yes | maybe | no

3. Cook with peace of mind

Date __/__/____

Place _____

Description of the moment _____

_____

_____

_____

Liking

Unforgettable Photo

it Again? | yes | maybe | no |

4. Bike Trip

Date __/__/____

Place _____

Description of the moment _____

_____

_____

_____

Liking

Unforgettable Photo

it Again? | yes | maybe | no |

5. Visit to a Museum

Date __/__/____

Place _____

Description of the moment _____

_____

_____

_____

Liking

Unforgettable Photo

it Again?   yes   maybe   no

6. Dance Lesson

Date __/__/____

Place _____

Description of the moment _____

_____

_____

_____

Liking

Unforgettable Photo

it Again? | yes | maybe | no

7. Mountain Hike

Date __/__/____

Place _____

Description of the moment _____

_____

_____

_____

Liking

Unforgettable Photo

it Again? | yes | | maybe | | no |

8. Day at the beach

Date __/__/____

Place _____

Description of the moment _____

_____

_____

_____

Liking

Unforgettable Photo

it Again? | yes | maybe | no |

9. Karaoke Evening

Date __/__/____

Place _____

Description of the moment _____

_____

_____

_____

Liking

Unforgettable Photo

it Again? | yes | maybe | no |

10. Look at the Stars

Date __/__/____

Place _____

Description of the moment _____

_____

_____

_____

Liking

it Again? | yes | maybe | no |

11. Photograph Anything

Date __/__/____

Place ....

Description of the moment ....

....

....

....

Liking

Unforgettable Photo

it Again? | yes | | maybe | | no |

12. Board Game

Date __/__/____

Place _____

Description of the moment _____

_____

_____

_____

Liking

Unforgettable Photo

it Again? | yes | maybe | no |

13. Wellness Day

Date __/__/____

Place _____

Description of the moment _____

Liking

Unforgettable Photo

it Again? yes maybe no

14. Romantic Dinner

Date __/__/____

Place _____

Description of the moment _____

_____

_____

_____

Liking

Unforgettable Photo

it Again? | yes | maybe | no |

15. Visit to a Farm

Date __/__/____
Place _____
Description of the moment _____
_____
_____
_____

Liking

Unforgettable Photo

it Again? | yes | maybe | no

16. Walk in the Woods

Date __/__/____

Place _____

Description of the moment _____

_____

_____

_____

Liking

Unforgettable Photo

it Again? | yes | | maybe | | no |

17. Day at the Luna park

Date __/__/____

Place ....

Description of the moment ....

....

....

....

Liking

Unforgettable Photo

it Again? | yes | maybe | no |

18. Breakfast in Bed

Date __/__/____

Place _____

Description of the moment _____

_____

_____

_____

Liking

Unforgettable Photo

it Again? | yes | maybe | no

19. Reading Evening

Date __/__/____

Place ....

Description of the moment ....
....
....
....

Liking

Unforgettable Photo

it Again? | yes | maybe | no |

20. Shopping Day

Date __/__/____

Place _____

Description of the moment _____

_____

_____

_____

Liking

Unforgettable Photo

it Again? | yes | maybe | no |

21. Go to the Gym

Date __/__/____

Place _____

Description of the moment _____

Liking

Unforgettable Photo

it Again? | yes | | maybe | | no |

22. Day at the Fair

Date __/__/____

Place _____

Description of the moment _____

_____

_____

_____

Liking

Unforgettable Photo

it Again? | yes | maybe | no |

23. Make a Puzzle

Date __/__/____

Place _____

Description of the moment _____

Liking

Unforgettable Photo

it Again? | yes | maybe | no

24. Boat Ride

Date __/__/____

Place _____

Description of the moment _____

_____

_____

_____

Liking

Unforgettable Photo

it Again? | yes | | maybe | | no |

25. Gardening

Date __/__/____

Place _____

Description of the moment _____

Liking

Unforgettable Photo

it Again?   yes   maybe   no

26. Stay up late

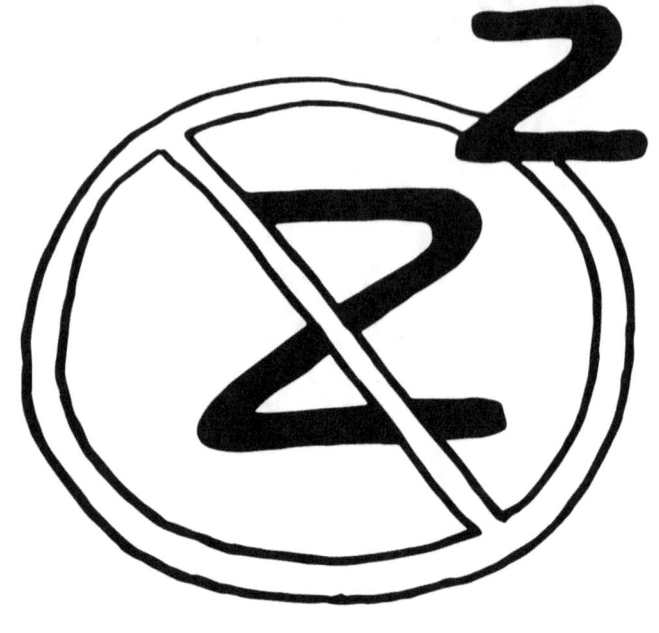

Date __/__/____

Place _____

Description of the moment _____
_____
_____
_____

Liking

Unforgettable Photo

it Again? | yes | | maybe | | no |

27. Cooking Lesson

Date __/__/____

Place _____

Description of the moment _____

Liking

Unforgettable Photo

it Again? | yes | maybe | no

28. Do House Cleaning

Date __/__/____

Place _____

Description of the moment _____

_____

_____

_____

Liking

Unforgettable Photo

it Again? | yes | maybe | no |

29. Evening at the Theatre

Date __/__/____

Place ....

Description of the moment ....

....

....

....

Liking

Unforgettable Photo

it Again? | yes | maybe | no |

30. Eat a quiet Ice cream

Date __/__/____

Place _____

Description of the moment _____

_____

_____

_____

Liking

Unforgettable Photo

it Again? | yes | maybe | no |

31. Wine Tasting

Date __/__/____

Place _____

Description of the moment _____

_____

_____

_____

Liking

Unforgettable Photo

it Again? | yes | maybe | no |

32. Train despite your Age

Date __/__/____

Place _____

Description of the moment _____

_____

_____

_____

Liking

Unforgettable Photo

it Again? | yes | maybe | no |

33. go to Cultural festival

Date __/__/____

Place _____

Description of the moment _____

_____

_____

_____

Liking

Unforgettable Photo

it Again? | yes | maybe | no |

34. Quiz Night

Date __/__/____
Place _____
Description of the moment _____
_____
_____
_____

Liking

Unforgettable Photo

it Again? | yes | maybe | no |

35. Pay the bills Yourself

Date __/__/____

Place _____

Description of the moment _____

_____

_____

_____

Liking

Unforgettable Photo

it Again? | yes | maybe | no |

36. Mountain Bike

Date __/__/____

Place _____

Description of the moment _____

_____

_____

_____

Liking

Unforgettable Photo

it Again? | yes | maybe | no |

37. Coffee at the Bar

Date __/__/____

Place ....

Description of the moment ....
....
....
....

Liking

Unforgettable Photo

it Again? | yes | maybe | no |

38. Don't set the Alarm

Date __/__/____

Place _____

Description of the moment _____

_____

_____

_____

Liking

Unforgettable Photo

it Again? | yes | maybe | no |

39. Spend more with Family

Date __/__/____

Place _____

Description of the moment _____

_____

_____

_____

Liking

Unforgettable Photo

it Again? | yes | maybe | no

40. City Tour

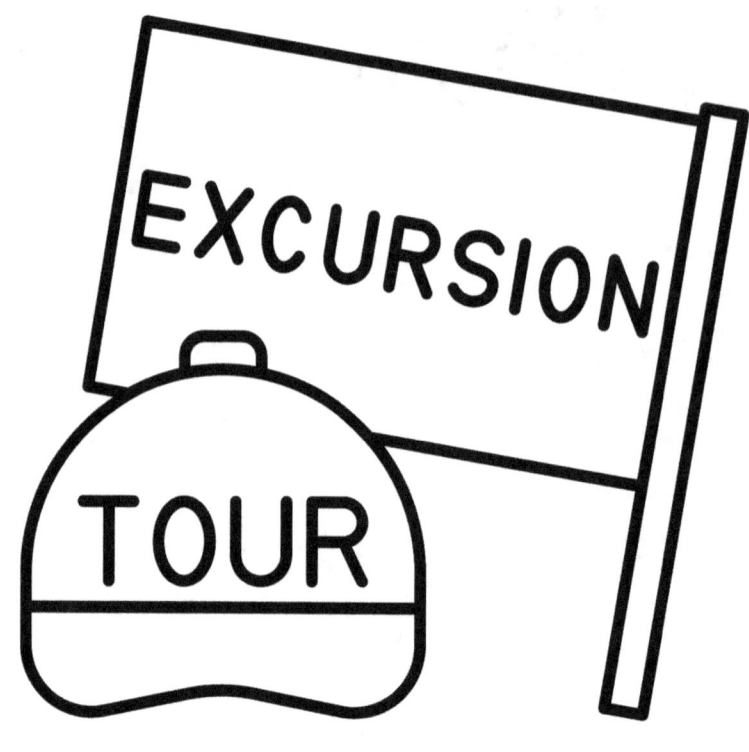

Date __/__/____

Place _____

Description of the moment _____

_____

_____

_____

Liking

Unforgettable Photo

it Again? | yes | maybe | no

41. Watch a Movie late at night

Date __/__/____

Place ....

Description of the moment ....

....

....

....

Liking

Unforgettable Photo

it Again? | yes | | maybe | | no |

42. Motorbike Trip

Date __/__/____

Place _____

Description of the moment _____

_____

_____

_____

Liking

Unforgettable Photo

it Again? yes maybe no

43. Fishing Day

Date __/__/____
Place _____
Description of the moment _____
_____
_____
_____

Liking

Unforgettable Photo

it Again? | yes | maybe | no |

44. Horseback Excursion

Date __/__/____
Place _____
Description of the moment _____
_____
_____
_____

Liking

Unforgettable Photo

it Again? | yes | | maybe | | no |

45. Plan a Surprise

Date __/__/____

Place _____

Description of the moment _____

_____

_____

_____

Liking

Unforgettable Photo

it Again? | yes | maybe | no

46. visit a Waterfall

Date __/__/____

Place _____

Description of the moment _____

_____

_____

_____

Liking

Unforgettable Photo

it Again? | yes | | maybe | | no |

47. Snorkelling Day

Date __/__/____

Place _____

Description of the moment _____

Liking

Unforgettable Photo

it Again? | yes | | maybe | | no |

48. Castle Tours

Date __/__/____

Place _____

Description of the moment _____

_____

_____

_____

Liking

Unforgettable Photo

it Again? | yes | maybe | no

49. day of Fooling around

Date __/__/____

Place ....

Description of the moment ....

....

....

....

Liking

Unforgettable Photo

it Again? | yes | maybe | no |

50. afternoon of Pampering

Date __/__/____

Place _____

Description of the moment _____
_____
_____
_____

Liking

Unforgettable Photo

it Again? | yes | maybe | no |

51. Play Cards

POKER

Date __/__/____

Place _____

Description of the moment _____

_____

_____

_____

Liking

Foto Indimenticabili

it Again? | yes | maybe | no |

52. love on the washing machine

Date __/__/____

Place _____

Description of the moment _____

_____

_____

_____

Liking

Unforgettable Photo

it Again? | yes | maybe | no |

53. Create a Scrapbook

Date __/__/____

Place ....

Description of the moment ....

....

....

....

Liking ♡ ♡ ♡ ♡ ♡

Unforgettable Photo

it Again?   yes   maybe   no

54. Fill out this Diary

Date __/__/____

Place _____

Description of the moment _____

_____

_____

_____

Liking

Unforgettable Photo

it Again? | yes | maybe | no

55. Online Games

Online

Date __/__/____

Place _____

Description of the moment _____

_____

_____

_____

Liking ♡♡♡♡♡

Unforgettable Photo

it Again? | yes | | maybe | | no |

56. Gondola in Venice

Date __/__/____

Place _____

Description of the moment _____

_____

_____

_____

Liking

Unforgettable Photo

it Again? | yes | maybe | no |

57. Parigi, Torre Eifelle

Date __/__/____

Place _____

Description of the moment _____

_____

_____

_____

Liking

Unforgettable Photo

it Again? | yes | maybe | no

58. Amsterdam Canals

Date __/__/____

Place _____

Description of the moment _____

_____

_____

_____

Liking

Unforgettable Photo

it Again?   yes   maybe   no

59. Santorini, Grecia

Date __/__/____

Place --

Description of the moment ------------------------

Liking

Unforgettable Photo

it Again? | yes | maybe | no |

60. Versaille Garden

Date __/__/____

Place _____

Description of the moment _____

_____

_____

_____

Liking

Unforgettable Photo

it Again? | yes | maybe | no |

61. Vienna Markets

Date __/__/____

Place _____

Description of the moment _____

Liking

Unforgettable Photo

it Again? | yes | | maybe | | no |

62. Romantic dinner in Prague

Date __/__/____

Place _____

Description of the moment _____

Liking

Unforgettable Photo

it Again? | yes | maybe | no |

63. Dinner on the Danudio

Date __/__/____

Place _____

Description of the moment _____

_____

_____

_____

Liking ♡ ♡ ♡ ♡ ♡

Unforgettable Photo

it Again? | yes | maybe | no |

64. Paella in Barcellona

Date __/__/____

Place _____

Description of the moment_____

_____

_____

_____

Liking

Unforgettable Photo

it Again? | yes | maybe | no |

65. have a Beer in Dublino

Date __/__/____

Place _____

Description of the moment _____

_____

_____

_____

Liking

Unforgettable Photo

it Again? | yes | | maybe | | no |

66. Take a Photo in Lisbon

Date __/__/____

Place _____

Description of the moment _____

_____

_____

_____

Liking

Unforgettable Photo

it Again? | yes | maybe | no |

67. Maldives beach

Date __/__/____

Place _____

Description of the moment _____

_____

_____

_____

Liking

Unforgettable Photo

it Again? | yes | maybe | no |

68. Nile Cruise

Date __/__/____

Place _____

Description of the moment _____
_____
_____
_____

Liking

Unforgettable Photo

it Again? | yes | | maybe | | no |

69. Grand Canyon

Date __/__/____

Place _____

Description of the moment _____

Liking

Unforgettable Photo

it Again? | yes | | maybe | | no |

70. Machu Picchu, Perù

Date __/__/____

Place _____

Description of the moment_____

_____

_____

_____

Liking

Unforgettable Photo

it Again? yes maybe no

71. Red square in Moscow

Date __/__/____

Place _____

Description of the moment _____

Liking

Unforgettable Photo

it Again?   yes   maybe   no

72. Evening in Dubai Marina

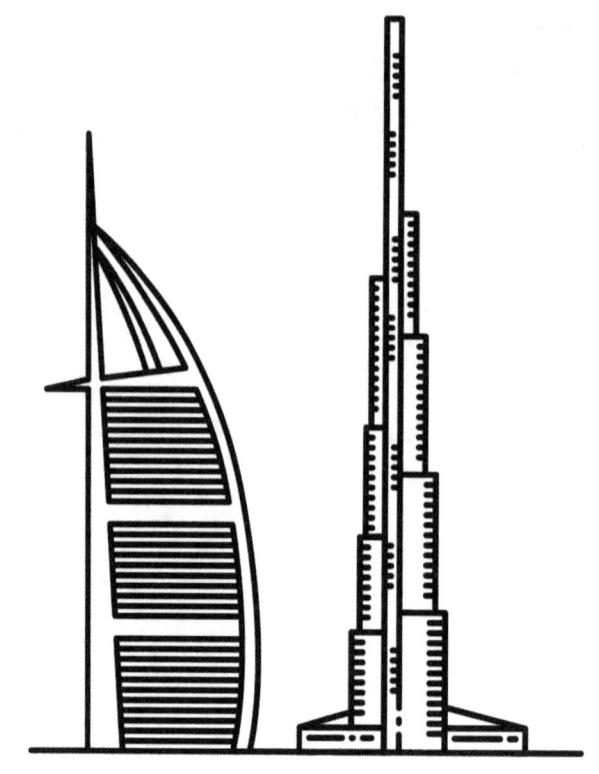

Date __/__/____

Place _____

Description of the moment _____

_____

_____

_____

Liking

it Again? yes maybe no

73. hot air Balloon in Türkiye

Date __/__/____

Place _____

Description of the moment _____

_____

_____

_____

Liking

Unforgettable Photo

it Again? | yes | | maybe | | no |

74. sunset in Hawaii

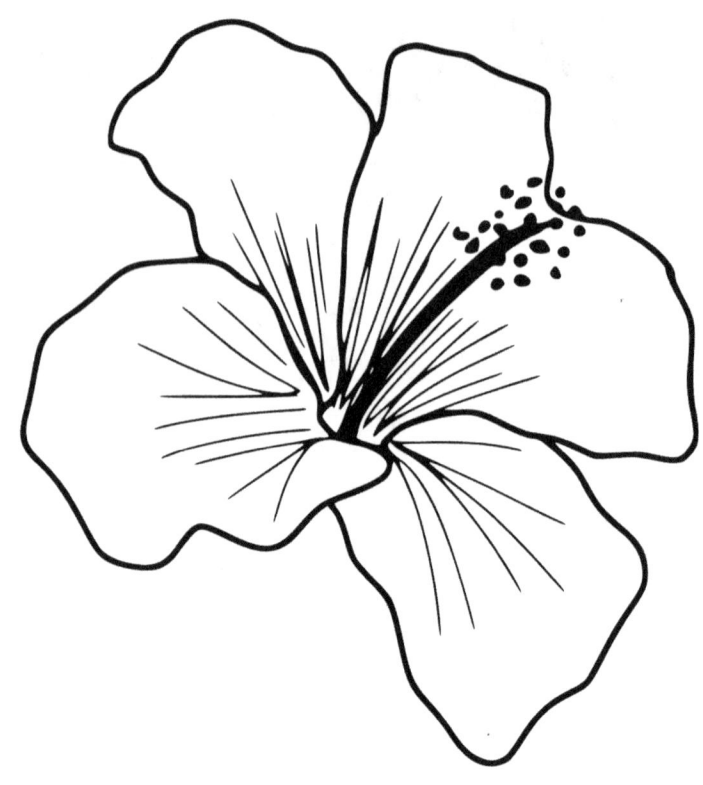

Date __/__/____

Place ....

Description of the moment ....

....

....

....

Liking

Unforgettable Photo

it Again? | yes | maybe | no |

75. Safari in Kenia

Date   _ _ / _ _ / _ _ _ _

Place _____

Description of the moment _____

_____

_____

_____

Liking 

Unforgettable Photo

it Again? | yes | | maybe | | no |

76. temples in Thailand

Date __/__/____

Place _____

Description of the moment _____

_____

_____

_____

Liking

Unforgettable Photo

it Again? | yes | maybe | no |

77. Christmas lunch

Date __/__/____

Place _____

Description of the moment _____

Liking

Unforgettable Photo

it Again? | yes | maybe | no

78. sleep late in the morning

Date __/__/____
Place ....
Description of the moment ....
....
....
....

Liking

Unforgettable Photo

79. Buy a House

Date __/__/____

Place _____

Description of the moment _____

_____

_____

_____

Liking

Unforgettable Photo

it Again? | yes | | maybe | | no |

80. Adopt a Puppy

Date __/__/____

Place _____

Description of the moment _____

_____

_____

_____

Liking

Unforgettable Photo

it Again? | yes | | maybe | | no |

A Wish For a Lot Of Happiness

I remind you that if you liked the book , the biggest help you can give me is a review on AMAZON.

Thanks again for purchasing my book,
the result of a lot of work.
I hope to see you again for future purchases
and you could share
this new retiree activity book
with those you love.

www.ingramcontent.com/pod-product-compliance
Lightning Source LLC
Chambersburg PA
CBHW062321220526
45469CB00008B/2590